HOW TO KNOW YOU ARE GOING TO HEAVEN

A PROFESSOR

of philosophy in a university was lecturing on the lack of certainty in our age. "Certainty is impossible," he said. "We can know nothing for certain."

A freshman raised her hand and asked "Professor, are you sure of that?"

"I'm certain!" he replied.

Yes, we live in an age of uncertainty. We're learning more and more about everything and yet we seem to know less and less for sure.

KNOW WHAT YOU KNOW

In contrast, the first followers of Jesus were characterized by their certainty. They didn't guess . . . or hope . . . or wish. They knew for certain. They were even willing to die for that certainty!

They said, "We know that our sins are forgiven. We know that we are the children of God. We know that to die is to be present with the Lord. We know that nothing can separate us from the love of God which is in Christ Jesus, our Lord."

Unfortunately, most people don't have such confidence when it comes to eternal life. They hope, they wish, they would like to think, but they don't know for certain. As a result, they have no confidence in the face of death, which is tied to the certainty that

DO YOU HAVE CERTAINTY ABOUT ETERNITY? DO YOU KNOW FOR SURE?

Do you have certainty about eternity? Do you know for sure?

Throw away all trust in your own goodness. Look to the cross of Jesus Christ. See him who suffered the agony of the condemned in your place, who received from his own Father the penalty we deserve and then rose from the dead. Christ himself "bore our sins in his body on the tree [cross]" (1 Peter 2:24). Transfer all of your hopes from what you have done to what he has done for you at Calvary. Place your trust in him alone. "Whoever has the Son has life; whoever does not have the Son of God does not have life. I write these things to you who believe in the name of the Son of God that you might know that you have eternal life" (1 John 5:12–13).

Do you know that you have eternal life?

DR. D. JAMES KENNEDY

Here's a suggested prayer:

Lord Jesus Christ, I know I am a sinner and do not deserve eternal life. But, I believe you died and rose from the grave to purchase a place in heaven for me. Lord Jesus, come into my life; take control of my life; forgive my sins and save me. I repent of my sins and now place my trust in you for my salvation. I receive the free gift of eternal life.

To read the Bible, learn about Jesus, or find a church in your area, visit **Crossway.org/LearnMore**.

www.goodnewstracts.org